Contents

Butterfly

Butterflies fly by day.
Their feelers have knobs.
They rest with their
wings closed.

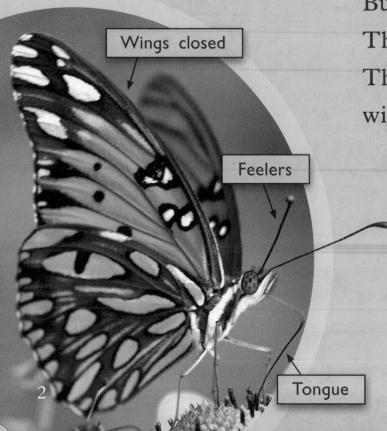

Wings closed

Feelers

Tongue

Curled
tongue

Butterfly

2

Moth

Moths fly at night.
Their feelers are feathery.
They rest with their
wings open.

Feelers

Wings open

What's the Same?

They can both curl up
their tongue. They both
drink **nectar** from flowers.
They are both insects.

3

Frog

Most frogs have
wet skin. It is smooth.
They have long
back legs.

4

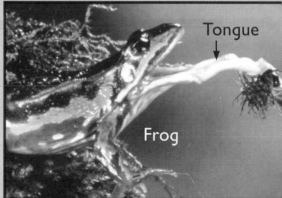

Tongue

Frog

Toad

Most toads have
dry skin. It is bumpy.
They have short
back legs.

What's the Same?

They both have a long,
sticky tongue for
catching food. They
are both **amphibians**.

Crocodile

Crocodiles have a narrow, pointed snout. Their upper and lower teeth stick out of their jaws. Crocodiles are a light tan color.

Teeth

Snout

← Eye

Crocodile

6

Alligator

Alligators have a short, wide snout. Their bottom teeth fit into holes in their upper jaw. Alligators are grayish black in color.

Snout

Teeth

What's the Same?

They both have eyes on top of their head. They are both **reptiles**.

Cheetah

Cheetahs have black lines from their eyes called tear lines. They have solid black spots on their coat. They hunt by day. They can run fast.

Tear lines

Cheetah's coat

8

Leopard

Leopards do not have tear lines.
Leopards have black rings
on their coat. They hunt
by night. They are
good climbers.

Leopard's coat

What's the Same?

They both hunt and eat
other animals. They are
predators. They are
both big cats.

9

Tail →

Monkey

Monkeys are tree lovers. They run along branches on all fours. Some monkeys swing by their long tail.

Monkeys

10

Ape

In trees, apes swing from branches by their strong arms. Apes do not have a tail at all!

What's the Same?

Both animals live in groups. They are both **primates**.

11

Bee

Bees have a short, wide body. Bees can sting only once. Then they die. Bees make honey.

12

Bee's nest

Wasp

Wasps have a long, thin body. They can sting many times. Wasps do not make honey.

What's the Same?

Bees and wasps build nests. They live in large groups. They are both insects.

13

Don't Be Fooled!

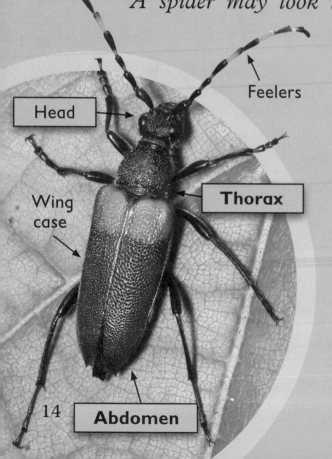

A spider may look like an insect. But look closer.

Feelers

Head

Wing case

Thorax

Abdomen

Insect

Insects have six legs.

Their body has three parts.

Insects have feelers.

They also have wings.

Beetle eggs

Spider

Spiders have eight legs.
Their body has
only two parts.
Spiders do not have
feelers or wings.

What's the Same?

Their young hatch
from eggs.

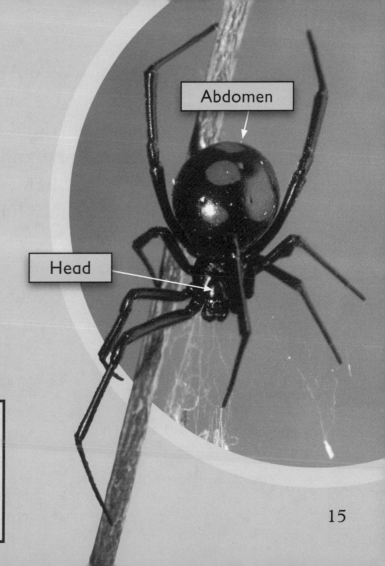

Abdomen

Head

15

Glossary

abdomen the back part of an insect or a spider's body

amphibian a cold-blooded animal that lives in water when it is young and on land when it is an adult

nectar a sweet liquid found inside flowers

predator an animal that hunts and eats other animals

primate a group of animals that includes apes, monkeys, and lemurs

reptile a cold-blooded animal with scaly skin, such as a snake, turtle, lizard, or alligator

thorax the middle part of an insect's body

Index